NEW CAR

Kate Petty

Photographs by Ed Barber

Start to Finish

Contents

A & C Black · London

The changing shape of cars

A car costs thousands of pounds. For most people a 'new car' is a second-hand one. For others, it is a car with the latest registration number. But for the car makers, a 'new car' is a new design, based on new ideas and often with a new name.

Volkswagen Beetle (1953)

Model T Ford (1923)

The first cars were built nearly a hundred years ago and looked very like the horse-drawn carriages of the time. Modern cars have become much more comfortable, and can go faster. Gradually, the shapes of cars have become smoother and more streamlined. Now, there is not so much difference between different makes of car. Why do you think this is?

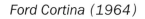

Ford Cortina (1964)

Car manufacturers usually produce a range of different-sized cars aimed at different sorts of people. Nowadays, when they bring out a new car, it is often a slightly altered version of a car that came before it. The Ford Fiesta was the first small car that Ford produced for many years. It appeared in 1976 but there have been several new versions since then.

Austin Mini (1959)

Who has the first ideas?

The very first discussions about a new car take place between the directors of the company, years before the car is made. In a big international company, directors from different countries can join in the meeting using satellite television.

A new car costs millions of pounds to design and make so the directors want to be as sure as possible that people will buy it. A market research team asks people questions about the way they live and the sort of transport they need – do they want fast expensive cars or small economical cars which do less harm to the environment? The company looks closely at other cars which sell well – what makes them popular? Finally they start to make plans for the new car.

Using the market research, the product planning department makes a list of things the new car must have.

The designers use this list to produce lots of different drawings.

Simon is a designer. He sketches lots of different ideas for the new car.

Simon also draws on a special computer with a high definition screen, which means his drawings look almost three-dimensional. He uses a light pen to sketch his ideas. At the touch of a button, he can choose any of six million different colours.

Choosing the right design

Designing a new car can take months or even years. The designers meet with the marketing department to talk about their ideas. They narrow the choice to about four or five different versions. Then they start work on all the parts.

In the CAD/CAM (Computer Aided Design/Computer Aided Manufacturer) department, a computer is used to design the working parts of the car, such as the steering wheel. The designer can look at a section of the wheel close-up, and make sure that the size is right for the new car. The computer can make parts look bigger or smaller, or show a different section.

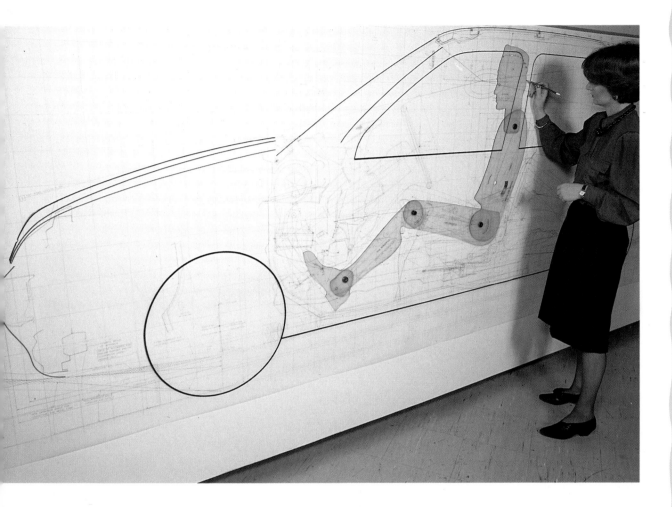

Engineers designing the car body produce accurate life-size diagrams of the car. They draw around flat plastic shapes of people, to check that the car will be comfortable. For example, the designer can move the leg shapes to make sure the car will have enough leg room.

The next stage is to make a 'tape rendering' of the new car. This is a full-size picture of the car made with sticky tape. The designers can show people what the car will look like, and can make any necessary changes by moving the sticky tape.

Inside the car

When it comes to selling the new car, the interior design of the car is as important as the outside. The designers must take as much care with the small details, such as the door handles and seat belts, as with the larger parts of the car.

The designers look at different kinds of seat to try to decide what will be fashionable in five years time, when the car will first be sold. They start with sketches, then build a wooden car so that they can experiment with the inside. They also use it to check that the inside and outside work well together.

Janine is a textile designer. She is in charge of choosing the colours and material used to cover the seats.

The textile designer looks at fashions and magazines to choose the colours for the fabric. Then she talks to suppliers to get just the colours and textures she wants to go with the car's paintwork. She usually chooses quiet colours rather than bright fluorescent ones. Why do you think this is?

Making models

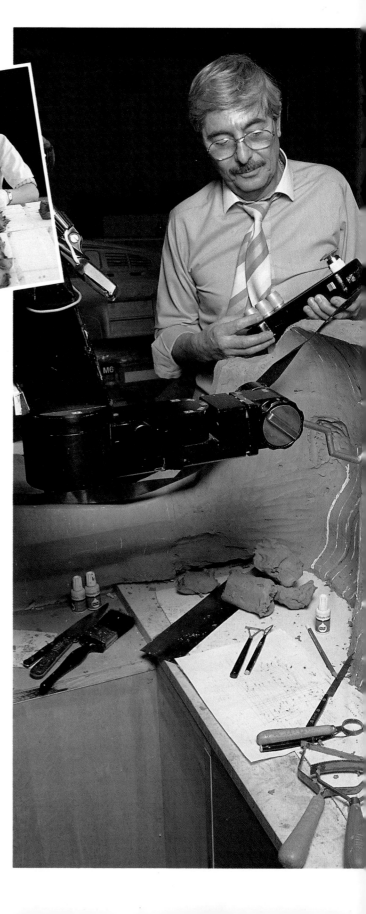

The wooden car is shown to other people in the company and some changes are made. But the best way to get a real idea of how the new car will look is to make a detailed full-sized model. The models are made by hand out of clay. The clay modellers are very skilled; when the model is finished and painted, it looks just like a real car.

Clay models are built of all the different versions of the car before an acceptable design is agreed on. The company discuss them all and show them to lots of people. They compare them with other small cars made by their competitors. Finally they decide which one they are going to make. The designers then concentrate on just one version. Up until this point the car just has a code name, but now it is given its proper name. Some of the early suggestions of names for the Fiesta were Amigo, Strada and Pony.

The full-sized clay model is scanned with a sharp tool which sends the measurements to be stored on a computer. These will be used to make the final version of the car. Alterations can still be made to the clay model. Once the design is less likely to be altered, models are made from fibreglass.

Models of the new car are used for testing. One test is to put the model car in a wind tunnel where smoky air is blown over it by fans. Patterns in the smoke show how smoothly the car will cut through the air as it travels. Finished cars are also tested in this way.

Moving parts

The new car is beginning to look good, but will it go? Development engineers build and test the engine and all the other moving parts of the car. They also use computer pictures to see how some moving parts will behave when the car is driven. It can take up to seven years for a new engine to be developed.

The prototype engines are thoroughly tested. Some are run until they break down to see how long it takes.

One test allows the engineer to see how much fuel an engine uses. The prototype engine is connected to a machine which simulates the effects of being driven. The results for each engine are recorded on a test sheet.

Real cars are needed for some tests, so prototype cars are built by hand. The engineers must try many different safety tests on the new car. They need to know what will happen if there is a crash.

These dummies are the same size and weight as real people. They are strapped in and the car is catapulted at great speed along a track to simulate an accident. Instruments on the dummies and a high-speed camera record the results of the test.

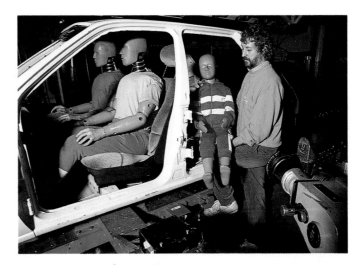

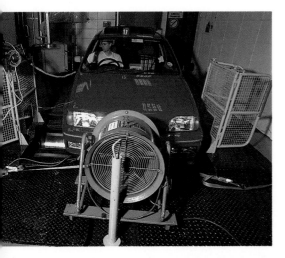

Prototype cars are also used for an 'emissions' test. While the car engine is run, all the gases that come out of the exhaust pipe are collected and measured. The car is connected to a computer. The print-out and the gases are analysed.

Other tests are carried out on a test track. The cars are driven on all kinds of different surfaces, such as cobbles and wet roads. As the new car moves nearer to production, the factory produces some prototypes to try out the new machines which are needed to make the car. For two years before the car goes on sale, prototypes are shown to thousands of potential future customers.

The engine plant

At last the final designs are approved, the prototype tests are completed and the factory is ready to begin mass producing the car.

The engines are made separately from the bodies. First, empty engine blocks arrive at the factory. They are washed and put on a conveyor belt which carries them along the assembly line. As they travel along, different parts of the engine are added. First the pistons are put in place. They will help to make the wheels move.

Some parts are put in place by robots and some by skilled operators. The conveyor belt is seven kilometres long. The clutch is one of the last things to be added.

Every engine is run for twelve minutes to test that it works. Then it is packed up ready to be fitted to the rest of the car.

The press shop

At the press shop, the metal panels which form the body of the car are cut and shaped.

Thin lengths of metal are fed into the press. The press, which weighs as much as 150 double-decker buses, stamps each piece into the shape of a car door. The off-cuts drop into a pit where they can be gathered up and recycled.

The pieces move on automatically through different sections of the press. The window areas are stamped out so that glass can later be fitted. Every hour, one of the pieces is checked to make sure the machine is doing its job properly.

The panels are collected at the end and stacked in racks, ready to be fitted together.

Making the body

In the body assembly area of the factory, conveyor belts carry parts along the factory floor. The first stage of assembly is to fix the sides of the body to the underneath. Operators tack the sides on using small metal tabs which they tap into place with hammers. Now the car has a shape.

The shell of the car is held in a clamp while robots join the pieces together permanently. They weld the metal by heating it to such a high temperature that the pieces melt together. The robots get their instructions from a code, so they can tell if they are welding a three-door or five-door car, or a van. Next the doors and boot lids are attached.

Quality control takes place at every stage.

Colin checks the car bodies. He marks any little faults with magnetic arrows and chalk. They will be corrected before the car moves on to be painted.

The conveyor belt carries the car bodies for one and a half kilometres over a bridge between the assembly factory and the paint shop.

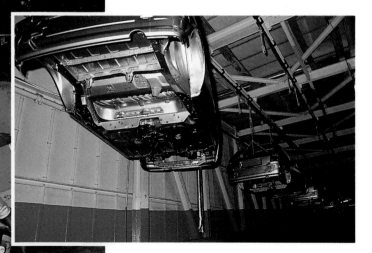

The paint shop

As the car body passes into the paint shop, a bill tag with a description is fixed on to it. Every single car being made has been ordered by a customer who has chosen the colour and the type. This car is going to be a red British one, with a right-hand drive. Red is the most popular car colour in Britain. Other Europeans prefer white cars.

The car body is steam-cleaned in a giant car-wash and then dipped in a bath of liquid metal to protect it against rust. It is sealed and given an undercoat, which is baked on. The surface is sanded and the dust removed with dusters made from ostrich feathers.

Now the car body is ready to receive the first of its seven coats of enamel paint. Robots spray a fine mist of paint over the car through nozzles that spin round 25 000 times a minute. The nozzles clean themselves every ten seconds. When the car is finished, the robots can use a different colour, following the computerized instructions they receive. So a white car can be painted immediately after a black one.

Operators in protective clothing spray the parts which the machines can't easily reach, such as the inside of the bonnet. Then the cars pass along the conveyor belt into ovens where the colour is baked on.

The engine meets the body

The production line journey continues. Next the dashboard, windows and other fittings are put in. Can you see the bar code on the side of the car? It matches the details on the checklists that have been stuck on the car and gives information about where the car will be delivered.

The back seats, lights and steering wheel are fitted. Then it is time for the car body to be lowered on to the engine. The computer makes sure that the right engine comes along the line at exactly the time its matching car body arrives on the conveyor belt.

Four operators carefully lower the body into position. Then, using high-powered tools, they fit the car together.

The car is nearly complete. On the last stages of the line, the wheels, windows, front seats, radio and windscreen wipers are installed.

Fit for the road

Four and a half litres of petrol are put in the tank, the oil and water are filled to the correct levels, and the new car can be started up for the very first time. Every day, one after another, 1 200 brand new vehicles roar into life and speed a short distance across the factory floor. Each one stops over a pit, where an operator checks the car from underneath.

Then it's on to the 'rolling road': rollers on which the car can run without going anywhere. The car spends half a minute on the rolling road. The lights come on, the horn beeps, and the windscreen washers spurt as each part is tested. The car accelerates and the steering, the speedometer, the brakes and the exhaust are all checked. The results are monitored at the front of the booth.

The car is now ready for the road. But its first journey is only as far as the distribution park. There, the new cars wait to be taken to the showrooms.

Transporting cars

Cars bound for Europe and other parts of the world can be loaded directly on to a ship, right next to the factory.

Railway tracks also run right through the factory site, so cars can be driven straight on to transporter trains. The number plates will not be fitted until the cars reach their destinations.

John's job is to load and drive a car transporter. His transporter carries twelve cars at a time.

Other cars are carried on car transporters. Each car is driven onto a ramp. The operator locks it firmly in place. Then he presses a remote control device which raises or lowers the ramp into position.

The showroom and after

The customer knows about the new Fiesta. She has seen it advertised in magazines and on the television. She has decided that this is the car that she likes and can afford.

When she buys the car, the dealer hands her the keys, and the documents which go with the car.

The best thing in your life?

Even we would have to admit that your car could never be the best thing in your life. Not even one of ours. But the next best thing, who knows? When a small car is as good as the new Ford Fiesta it could come a pretty close second.

We think it's the best small car in the world. Look at the new Fiesta LX featured here, just one of seven new Fiestas in the range. As you can see it's a brand new shape and it's now available with three or five doors.

Because it has a longer wheelbase and its wheels are wider apart, there's even more room inside than before. The boot is bigger, too, by 45%.

But outside, the new Fiesta remains a very compact car, so it's just as nippy around town as ever – big enough for comfort but small enough to park.

More power and anti-lock brakes. The car below has the latest 1.1 litre HCS engine (HCS stands for High Compression Swirl) which is 10% more powerful than before.

And can run on unleaded fuel without any adjustments.

It has a five speed gearbox as standard, which keeps down your revs at motorway speeds.

Or, if you drive a lot in traffic, and you have the five door version, you could order the CTX automatic. It's so efficient it gets to 60 mph

less than a secon
Another fe
models are also
lock brakes. You
them once, but yo
them if you do.
The best equip
Standard equip
includes the same
self-seek radio/cass
door mirrors, tinte
security door locks,
most Fiestas have e
never have been offe
before. Like the all
windscreen for fast e
front windows and ce
And, of course, yo
service and parts back
with owning a Ford. No
the Extra Cover Options
make you feel even more

Further informa
For more details of
Fiesta range from the Pos
exciting new fuel-injected Fie
soon, you can ring the Ford
Service free on 0800 01 01 10
still, you can call in and see
Fiestas at your nearest Ford
We think you'll agree, it's
small car in the w
Ford

The next best thing in your life?
The new Ford Fiesta. Ford

The dealer will look after any problems the car has, for the first year or so. This is useful for the customer, but also for the manufacturer who can use any information he receives to help with the design of future new cars. Any persistent problems can be corrected in designs for other cars.

Back in the design studio, another car, still under a code name, is well under way. Some designers look even further into the future with designs of cars that might be on the road in ten years time.

Do you think this is how cars might look in the twenty-first century?

A quick look at how a car is made

Ideas

Market research provides ideas for new cars.

Design

Several versions of the car are designed.

Interior Design

Type of seat etc, colour scheme and material chosen.

Testing

Prototype cars are built by hand and tested thoroughly.

Models

Full-size models of the cars made in clay and wood. One is chosen as the new Fiesta.

Showroom

Distribution Park

Orders delivered by ship,
railway and car transporter.

Advertising

Car advertised in
magazines and on
television.

Assembly

Engine lowered into body.
Minor fittings added.
All parts checked.

Paint Shop

Steam cleaning — anti-rust
treatment — undercoat — seven
coats of paint — baked dry.

Production

Engine assembled.
Metal body panels cut
and welded together.

Quality Control

Inspects every stage of
the production line.

Index

Published by A & C Black (Publishers) Limited
35 Bedford Row, London, WC1R 4JH

Text © 1991 Kate Petty
Photographs © 1991 Ed Barber

Acknowledgements

The author and publisher would like to thank everyone at Ford
Motor Company Limited who gave their time and expertise in
the preparation of this book, especially Mike Perry, Gordon
Royle, Victoria Hardisty and Jenny Heard. Also Jan Goode at
Dagenham Motors. The pictures of a Volkswagen Beetle
and an Austin Mini are reproduced by kind permission of the
National Motor Museum, Beaulieu. The pictures on p 2 (left),
p 3 (top), p 4, p 6 (top), p 10 (left), p 11, pp 20–21 (top) and
p 29 are reproduced by kind permission of Ford Motor
Company Limited.

A CIP catalogue record for this book
is available from the British Library.

ISBN 0–7136–3484 7

Filmset by August Filmsetting, Haydock, St Helens
Printed in Belgium by Proost International Book Production